The Little Tern

A Story of Insight

Tale by Brooke Newman
and illustrations by Lisa Mann Dirkes

HiddenSpring

First published in Great Britain by Simon & Schuster UK Ltd, 2001

ISBN 1-58768-016-5

Published in North America in 2001 by

HiddenSpring

an imprint of Paulist Press
997 Macarthur Boulevard
Mahwah, New Jersey 07430

www.hiddenspringbooks.com

Typeset by SX Composing DTP, Rayleigh, Essex
Printed and bound in Italy by
LEGO SpA

'Cheshire-Puss,' she began, rather timidly . . . 'Would you tell me please, which way I ought to go from here?'

'That depends a good deal on where you want to get to,' said the Cat.

'I don't much care where—' said Alice.

'Then it doesn't matter which way you go,' said the Cat.

Lewis Carroll

This is a story about an extraordinary little bird. And while undoubtedly most birds seem remarkable when considered on their individual merits, this particular bird was (one might venture to say) uniquely extraordinary.

The bird of this tale is a tern, more specifically, he is a Little Tern. The Little Tern is small, slender and a highly skilled acrobatic flier who spends most of his life in the air, soaring, diving, darting and hovering above the sea or inland rivers and lakes. Identified by his long narrow wings and a deeply forked tail, he has a yellow bill and a white wedge on his forehead. The Little Tern's short legs and small feet are not designed for spending much time on land. Indeed, the Little Tern is a land tourist, finding his home in the sky.

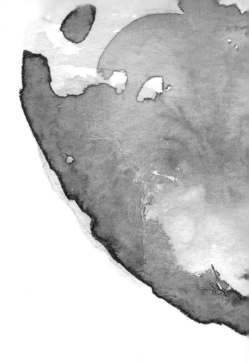

This story concerns the unique struggle faced by the Little Tern.

Throughout the telling of this tale the reader needs to recollect and be constantly mindful of the fact that the very quintessence of the tern is in his sky writings. What the tern knows and understands lies in paintings above the planet.

This now said, the struggle the tern faced can better be understood, since for some mysterious reason, he lost his ability to fly. This story recounts his journey through that most

discordant event. If ever there were a
circumstance that might have the potential for
turmoil, it surely would have to be one wherein
everything thought to be so turns out not to be
so, and all things known are at once unknown.

   Here then follows the story of this little Little
Tern and his struggle to retrieve what was lost.

The Story of the Little Tern

I was born during the season of the warming of the seas, when the light of each day stretches into the evening. My home was the forever sky above that blue-green sea. I spent most of my waking hours hovering above the ocean waiting for the slightest shadow to appear in the water below.

My days were quite fine and routine and when a chill set in the air I would join the other terns and travel southward for warmth. Our long flight was carefully designed by something greater than ourselves and with a direction deeply imbedded in our hearts and a timepiece in our souls, we would head towards a warmer place. And after some time passed we knew to take flight and return north. It was a good life, and wholly taken for granted.

However, one day this all changed. I stopped being able to fly and my life drastically changed. One day I was flying and the next I was not. What I had known was no longer there and what was before me seemed entirely unknown.

When something breaks it is necessary to repair it, so immediately I began to check myself for broken parts. Wings, feathers, feet, tail. I checked myself not once, but twice and more. I could find nothing broken nor missing. I could not find a single item to heal nor repair. I considered that there are things that get broken on the outside, like tails and wings, and things that get broken on the inside like beliefs and persuasions.

Naturally I concluded that what was broken must be on the inside, which at that very moment left me simply disheartened. Little Terns are, I thought, supposed to know one thing and one thing only — how to soar above the sea in search of shadows of fish below.

My flock regarded me with curiosity, and as they glided in for their smooth landings and positioned themselves by my side, they would question why I wasn't flying. Instead of simply telling them the truth — about which I was wholly uncertain — I concocted elaborate excuses. As time went on my excuses became inventions as I described beach adventures and discoveries of fine delicacies hidden in the sand.

So began my particular journey.

The Journey

During this time in my life I believed everything to have been lost and nothing to have remained of what I knew. All that I had known — my flock, the skies, my flights, my way — was no longer the same. What was before me was where I stood. What was ahead was completely mysterious. I longed for what had been and wondered where and why it might have vanished.

Therefore, this tale relates my journey on those very sands where the white dunes rise from the shoreline reaching toward the clouds and where lime-green grass paint-brushes the dunes' edges. During this period of my life I lived along the shoreline where the frequent morning fog rolled in off the waves, masking the land, the sea and the sky in one mist.

During those mornings I would listen to the familiar sound of the foghorn in the distant white lighthouse as it warned fishing boats at sea. These were the same fishing boats I once had followed into the harbour, alongside flocks of gulls, kittiwakes and terns diving for the remains of fish thrown overboard. I once competed for those morsels. That was then.

During this time I could only listen to the other birds' cries, the boats' drone hum, and the foghorn's song as I impatiently stood on shore.

For these reasons I naturally became a kind of collector on the beach. I collected colours, thoughts and dreams. At night I watched the skies unfold a magical twilight. These stars became companions and, indeed, I made acquaintance with quite a few good ones.

One particular star I had occasion to meet was hanging in the northeastern corner of the sky. It began to fall, as is common for stars every now and again, and then stopped short, began again and stopped short once again. I wondered why this star was so fickle.

I asked it, 'Why are you so fickle, Star?'

And it looked down, spotting me immediately, the way stars can so easily do, and responded, 'Fickle? Are you talking to me?'

'Yes, I am. I was watching you fall and stop and fall again and stop again.'

'Oh that. Yes, that is intentional. It is my job to check on the other stars.'

'Really?'

'Yes, really. And it is not an easy job. It takes a good eye and much patience, for there are many stars and they have a tendency to move around every now and again. A star changes through the years, and one that may have looked like that one million years ago, might look like this today.

'It is a time-consuming job that requires the ability to start and stop frequently,' the star said.

'What do you do with the information about the stars?'

'Do with it?'

'Yes, what is the purpose of checking on the stars?'

'Purpose?'

'Yes,' I asked.

'Purpose,' he mused. 'Well, I suppose it is to be a star, live like a star, and carry out the duties of a star. All things have a purpose.'

'Birds too?' I asked.

'Oh, absolutely. A bird's purpose is to be a bird.'

'What does that mean?' I asked disappointed.

'Well, truly I cannot say for a star can only know what it is that a star needs to do. I can watch a bird and make an educated guess, but honestly, a star will never completely know what it is to be a bird any more than a bird will fully understand the life of a star.'

And with that said the star disappeared into the dark night.

I saw the star many times again, but knowing how busy he was I decided against asking him any more questions. I considered what he had said and what he had left unsaid and found myself with few answers. In dismay I asked myself whether a bird without the ability to fly could still be called a bird.

If not a bird, then what was I? I was neither a
hippo, a rhino, a man, a gnat, a python or a rat.

Perhaps a bird could be a bird no matter where he was stationed about the planet. If a star fell to the ground, I reasoned, then it is still a star.

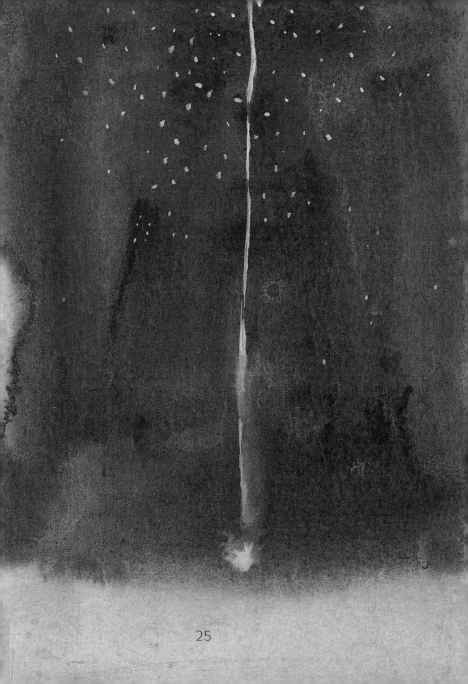

Winter, spring, summer and autumn passed
like this and with time I became an astute
student of the heavens and of the fragile edge
of the sea – the shoreline. I was as attentive to
the sea's edge as my fellow birds were to the

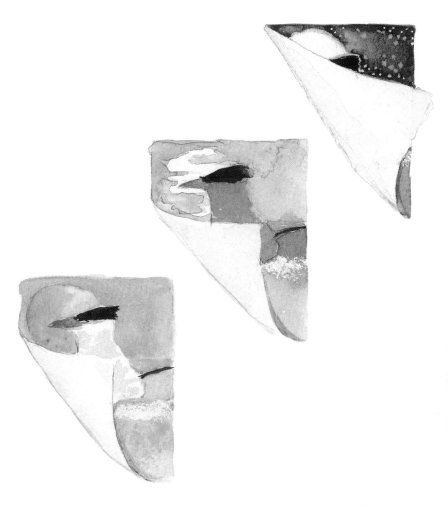

shadows at sea. I listened by day and by night to the waves breaking against the wet sands. I never gave up the hope that I would awaken to the skies, even though I lived on land.

One day I saw a purple flower growing in the sand. A flower is not supposed to grow in the sand.

I cautiously walked over to the flower, stood close, but not too close, to its soft petals, and greeted it with a nod. The flower did not respond. I didn't really expect that it would. It was a graceful flower and when a slight breeze drifted down the beach it swayed with the breeze. When, later that evening the fog settled in, the purple flower bathed in the mist.

At night, when the air became chilly, the flower bundled up its petals. I stood vigil over the flower all night.

In the morning I watched as the purple flower opened its petals.

I watched for differences to occur each day, hoping that within the differences I would find some answers. It occurred to me that within the seeming monotones there were vibrant colours. I then decided that up until now I had never truly seen anything in the monotones I had lived.

I had come to expect the tones I knew and surmise that they were relatively unimportant. Now however, I felt as if I were on the brink of being able to recognise that there was more to all these seeming monotones than a lack of colour.

I found leftovers and forgotten treasures on the beaches, particularly during the summer months. Crackers, biscuits, sour lemonade, peaches, raisins, crisps, apples. Buckets, pails, magazines, pencils, kites, balloons. I brought much of this back to my small retreat at the edge of the dune.

I collected tastes, smells, textures, words, dreams and thoughts, and mixed them as a painter might alongside sights, scenes and sensibilities. I ended up with a personal kaleidoscope that made my days and nights much kinder. And when I grew lonely I had the flower to visit.

Time passed slowly.

Though I had the purple flower to visit we did not converse, and after a while I began wishing for a friend. I assumed it would have to be quite an unusual creature to want to be a friend to such a strange bird as myself and considered dismissing the notion of friendship.

However, I surmised, it is exceedingly difficult to get what you want if you put it out of your mind.

Not too long after considering this need for a friend a quite surprising event occurred.

It was the break of dawn, the moment between darkness and daylight, when the sun first appears off in the distance, rising from below the sea's horizon. I was slowly making my way across the beach towards the shoreline when I noticed a small ghost crab standing motionless at the water's edge.

It seemed somehow appropriate that I should meet this peculiar creature. The ghost crab makes his home at the base of the dunes where he digs a deep hole in the sand. Every few hours he rushes from his shelter, crosses the wide

beach to the highest shoreline point, positions himself sideways to the sea, grips the sand, and waits for a wave to wash completely over him. Having thus gathered his meal and drink from that wave he then scurries back to his home at the foot of the dunes.

Friendship doesn't just come along in an instant. I knew that for us to become acquainted would take time. Particularly given our circumstances – he a crab and me a bird.

I would have to be patient ... something I was sorely unaccustomed to.

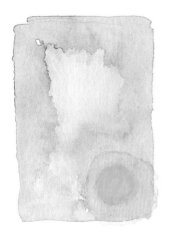 

The crab and I would keep an eye out for the other's movements, day by day.

I began to sing as I watched him on his beach run. I sang about the unending sky that began nowhere and went on forever.

I sang about the great waves that were born
far out to sea and somehow found their way to
shore.

As days passed we silently acknowledged each other.

One grey morning this changed. The ghost crab had wetted his gills at the shoreline and was returning across the sands toward his home when a seagull appeared overhead. The gull hovered preparing to swoop down for his prey, the crab.

Seeing this I cried out and made a terrible racket, rushed over to the crab's side, furiously kicked sand on to his shell, and so confused the gull that he flew off in search of an easier meal.

When the gull disappeared, the ghost crab
   dug out from beneath
    the mess I had made,
     looked up at me
      and I gazed down at him.

In this way, as many
      friendships are formed
        out of terrifying situations,

we became friends.

True friendship is a flower of very slow growing.

We stood side by side as the tide receded. A shoal appeared and water channels formed about the silk-smooth sand-bars. Minnows darted back and forth in the shallow waters. We observed quietly, and when the tide began to change my friend journeyed back towards the dune as I watched him protectively.

The next morning I watched as he made his way to the shoreline and then once again, quickly retreated to his home in the sand.

One day we found ourselves, quite by accident (or so it seemed), standing side by side at the water's edge. He sideways to the sea, me facing the horizon of the ocean.

We began to converse and I quickly told my history, my sorrow at not being able to fly, which

he acknowledged he had noticed and wondered about. I wanted to make this admission right away so that all things were out in the open, and if he were to reject me for this weakness or my honesty, then so be it. However, he simply dismissed this flaw, saying that it was unimportant in the realm of things. My friend the ghost crab was wise.

When I was done with my story, he simply said to me, 'The unusual is only unusual if you see it that way.'

'After all,' he continued, 'who better to applaud the unusual than me. Perhaps you are simply too accustomed to what you know and need to know what you do not know.'

I considered this silently and then he said, 'You have not lost the ability to fly, you have merely misplaced it.'

'How is that?' I asked.

'Losing a thing means it is lost and gone. Misplacing it is quite different. The thing you have misplaced is there, not lost. Finding it means paying attention to detail and recognising what it is you have not been recognising.'

'Like what?'

'Like things of import ... such as the things you have been collecting, which are the things important to collect.'

'The things I have collected are the things important to collect,' I repeated, trying to follow his very confusing way with words. I suppose it might be too much to expect from a ghost crab to speak in a simple, straightforward manner, considering their sideways nature.

We went our separate ways that evening and I could think of nothing but his words. The next morning I rose early to ask the ghost crab a million-and-one questions.

I waited patiently by the side of the sea for him to show, but he did not. I waited all day and into the night. He still did not show. When darkness was everywhere I grew anxious.

I considered that something dreadful might have happened to my strange sideways friend. I stood by the edge of the breaking waves, scanned the shoreline and looked far out to sea. No ghost crab was to be found.

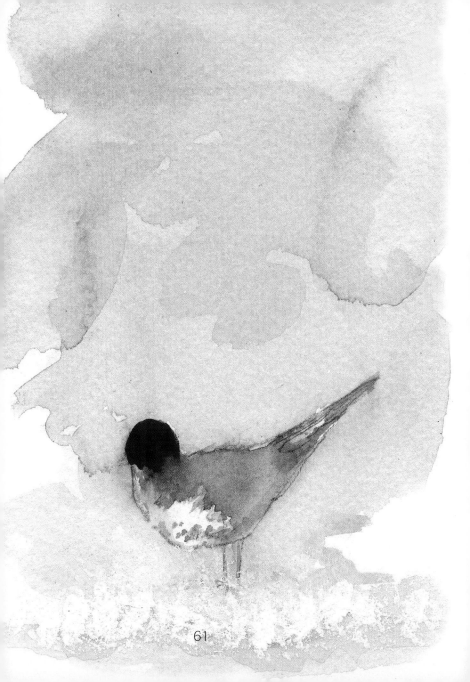

In the morning the fog rolled down the beach and I tried, in vain, to spot the ghost crab. I could see nothing but the surrounding greyness. The beach disappeared in the fog. It is indeed peculiar how you can see distances at one moment and see nothing at the next. I wondered if what you see disappears or is still there, but invisible?

Time slipped by.

A butterfly visited one morning.
He was most magnificent and his beauty took me by surprise. He rested on a delicate scallop shell that lay on the sand next to me.

As I watched the butterfly I considered that at night he was like the stars at day, there and yet invisible. I silently mused that beauty without a light shining upon it was ... what? If there were no light was the butterfly still beautiful?

I stopped waiting for the ghost crab to appear. Not that I wouldn't have been delighted to see him, but rather that I was no longer spending my days waiting. If asked why I had stopped waiting it would be difficult to say, except that I seemed to be terribly busy each day, studying, collecting, studying more, taking notice. It occurred to me that perhaps the ghost crab had intended that I discover the difference between waiting and wasting time, and waiting and learning from time.

One morning the sun rose and shone upon the beach and I noticed that my shadow was by my side. It must have been there before, but I had never noticed it before this morning. Peculiar how a thing can be there all the time and noticed none of the time.

At once, seeing the shadow seemed like a discovery. I likened it to finding a delicate sand dollar buried seaside. It is no easy task.

It is difficult.

It is difficult to find a sand dollar during a hurricane.

It is difficult to find one when the sun is shining very brightly.

It is difficult when the wind picks up.
It is difficult to find one when there is hail.

It is difficult when there is a high tide.
It is difficult when lightning strikes on the beach.

It is difficult when it is very cold.

It is difficult when it is very hot.

It is difficult when there are people on the beach.

It is difficult when there are many dogs on the beach.

Or horses.

Or sheep.

Or snakes.

Once found, though, a hard-to-find sand dollar — or a shadow for that matter — is far more valuable than if it were easy to come upon in the first place. It is remarkable, I thought, that this shadow had been there all along. Perhaps it wasn't lost so much as misplaced. This shadow that before seemed invisible, colourless, without purpose or true character now was magnificently resonant.

I considered the shadow . . . considered that a bird in flight does not have a shadow by his side. Only when he lands can he reflect upon that dark stretch of himself. A shadow is a reminder of what is there even when it is not there. Up until this time I had not taken notice of my shadow, or any shadow for that matter. A bird really cannot fly if he cannot see that his feathers and wings are truly worthy and magnificent. A bird needs to see the substance in all things beneath his wings in order to fly about the planet.

    Standing on the beach, I stared at my
shadow, noticed that the ghost crab had
appeared across the sand, at dune's edge. He
was watching me.
    Really that is quite amazing, I thought, that
something can be present without having a
presence.

And then, quite naturally, I raised and stretched my long wings into the breeze, and simply glided out over the shore's edge. I hovered above the break-water, watched as the white spray rose from the blue-green waves rolling on to themselves. I would now return to the skies as a bird who had finally seen his shadow. And indeed, as strange and alone as I had felt before, I was certain that this event must have happened to many birds before me and would happen again to others after. This is just how life unfolds for a bird in order that he is able to gain the wisdom needed to be a guardian of the sky.

Wings spread, I looked back to see my friend the ghost crab watching me. I knew we would meet again.

These watercolours are
For my parents and sister
Karen, my husband Jimmy
And children Christopher,
Hilary, Fred, Jimmy and
Maggie – gentle teachers
Of love and truth – renewers
Of spirit and joy.
And in memory of my dear
Friend Shelley.
'If a star fell to the
ground, I reasoned, it
is still a star.'
Little Tern

To my children
Nikos, Samantha, Blue, Joey
Who have taught me to
Appreciate the unexpected
And to Mark who has
Given me the courage
To expect it.
Not lastly,
To Huxley and Fleury
My hiking partners.

BROOKE NEWMAN has been the editor, co-author and author of numerous books, film scripts and plays. She received an award from the Pacific Northwest Writer's Guild for her one-act play, *My Mother's Lovers*. She lives in Aspen, Colorado with her four children and three dogs. LISA MANN DIRKES' career began as a freelance illustrator working for, among others, *Vogue*, but now focuses on fine art. She is married, with five children, and lives in Massachusetts.